+4.50

# ACKNOWLEDGMENT

GW00498813

The author gratefully acknowledges the assistance of Jonathan Evans, archivist, in providing access to the minutes of the House Committee and the annual reports of The London Hospital; for his help in the choice of illustrations, and in preparing the index and the text for publication.

Thanks are also offered to Sotiris Argyrou, John Blandy, Margaret Broadley, Claire Daunton and Maureen Scholes for their comments on the manuscript, and to Edith Parker for her support and patience in providing the word processing.

# H M The Queen
## Patron 1953 -

# FOREWORD

This is the story of the largest hospital in London, sited in the East End that has for centuries been the refuge of successive waves of immigrants escaping from political or religious persecution, usually poor, and often sick. No one is better fitted to tell this story than Sheila Collins. More than half a century of service in the ward and at the bedside has given her an insight which is the special prerogative of a nurse. She describes how The London began in the green-field site of Whitechapel, when there was still cholera in the streets and malaria in the marshes, and surgery was synonymous with pain and sepsis. She goes on to describe how, over the years The London managed to survive the recurrent threat of pestilence, enemy air raids, two Great Wars, and the no less dangerous perils of repeated political reorganisation.

The London has always had too many patients and too little money, but it has been rich in those who served it. Dr Collins tells the story of some of the more distinguished of the doctors, nurses and other staff who trained and worked in this building, many of them for generation after generation, making The London very much a huge family.

Today this great hospital is promised a major expansion and redevelopment which could bring wonderful opportunities and challenges in the coming century, and no doubt, some change. But one thing will not change. This will still be a happy hospital, whose glory lies not in the famous names of the past (though there have been many) or in its scientific and humanitarian achievement (although these have been great) but in a quality which is summed up in the phrase "an LH nurse", for all over the world this epitomises the essence of this hospital. Miss Eva Lückes referred to "the right spirit of Nursing, i.e. of active sympathy with suffering, manifested by unwearied kindness and unselfish devotion to the patients entrusted to her care". Margaret Broadley, another distinguished nurse, put it more simply - "patients come first".

John Blandy

"History can serve as a stimulus to action and an institution which ignores, or starts to forget, its history is in danger of losing its soul."
A.E. Clark Kennedy : The London, Pitman Medical 1963

# CONTENTS.

# INTRODUCTION.

The London Hospital received royal assent to its new title - The Royal London Hospital - when HM Queen Elizabeth II visited in July 1990 - the year of its 250th anniversary. The London Hospital, granted its royal charter in 1757 by George 11, has a long tradition of royal patronage. The first president, in 1742, was the Duke of Richmond, grandson of Charles II. He was succeeded in 1756 by Edward, Duke of York, and from then on this office was held by a member of the royal family - royal dukes, Queen Alexandra and Queen Mary. With the coming of the NHS in 1948, Queen Mary relinquished the office of president and became Patron. This tradition was followed by her grand daughter.

For more than two and a half centuries The London Hospital maintained its tradition of service to people from far afield, and to the local community for which it was established by its founders. Throughout the years of transition from a charitable institution founded for the poor, to a major teaching hospital in both the voluntary and the state system, the care of people with differing needs in vastly different social settings has remained paramount.

This brief history traces some of the outstanding achievements and events which shaped development in this changing world.

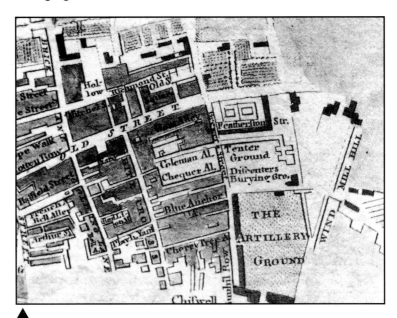

▲

*Featherstone Street, the first site c.1740*

# CHAPTER 1

# The Voluntary Hospital - 1740 - 1948

### Foundation - 1740 - 1840.

In the early eighteenth century London was a flourishing capital city with many families of wealth and power. Yet there were great social contrasts - poverty, starvation, inadequate water supplies and sanitation, and overcrowding. Public executions at Tyburn or tours of the madhouse, Bedlam, were amongst the sights of the city. Nevertheless there was a growing interest amongst the middle classes in practical philanthropy, as reformers stirred the social conscience. As a result several voluntary hospitals in London were founded. The London was the only one in the East End where in the latter part of the eighteenth century, the population was rapidly increasing by the drift of people from the countryside seeking work in the metropolis.

The London was founded on September 23rd. 1740 to "relieve the sick and ailing poor" by "seven ordinary men" led by a surgeon, John Harrison, who was a member of the Barber Surgeons' Company. These men meeting at the Feather's Tavern in Cheapside that autumn evening resolved to open a house in Featherstone Street at a rent of £15 p.a. in which they could accommodate 30 people. They had raised one hundred guineas between them, and determined therefore to seek further subscribers to maintain it. From amongst their number, Mr.Sclater was elected chairman, Fotherley-Baker, a lawyer, became treasurer, John Harrison became surgeon and Josiah Cole the apothecary. Weekly meetings were to be held and records were kept in a book with several columns to record :-

" the Names of the Patients, their Business and Place of Abode, Disorder, the Issue of the Case, and the Name of the Subscriber who sent them."

◄ The Foundation minute, 23rd September 1740,

*John Harrison, surgeon and founder,* ▲
*served the hospital for 13 years*

The London was founded
as a charity:-

" for relieving poor Manufacturers,
Sailors in the Merchants'
Service and their wives and children, with
medicine and advice in case of
sickness or accident".

Soon after the first patients were
admitted "there was only one shilling in
the bank" and hence a pressing need to
gain financial support. Subscriptions were
sought to maintain the charity, and
subscribers came from all walks of life.
Donors of 30 guineas as a lump sum
became life governors, those giving 5
guineas annually became governors with
the right to nominate persons for admission
by a letter signed by the governor a practice
which continued until 1898.

It soon became clear that the services
in the original house with 30 beds were
overstretched, and that larger premises
were needed.

A physician, Dr. Andrée M.D. of
Rheims, a Huguenot refugee, was appointed; he, with the apothecary, was to call at
the house each morning to see the sick,
and to order "medicines, plaisters and
ointments".
A married couple were engaged at £20 p.a.
to run the establishment, and, later as the
work developed, it was approved that :-

"Squire be contracted with by
the Chairman of the Committee
as a Nurse for the Womens' Ward
at the rate of £14 p.a."

*John Andrée, the first physician,* ▶
*served in office 24 years*

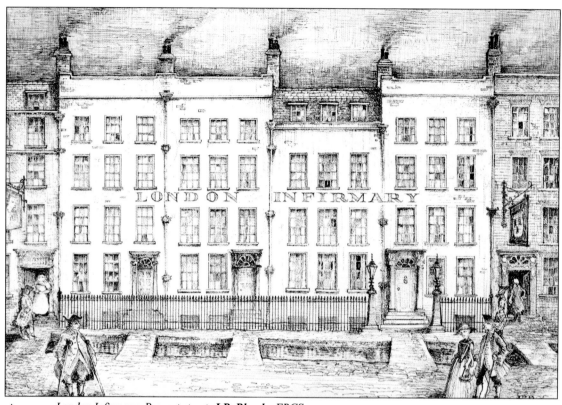

*London Infirmary, Prescot street* **J.P. Blandy** *FRCS.*
*The four houses provided beds in far from ideal conditions and were flanked by public houses*

The "London Infirmary" as it was then called, moved to a house in Prescot Street near the Tower in May 1741. Additional houses were acquired as they fell vacant and resources permitted. Within four years there were five houses and 68 beds - about this time the title was changed to London Hospital. Persistent insanitary conditions, a poor water supply, a leaking roof, and difficulties in sewage disposal forced the governors to consider moving the hospital. This was made even more necessary when the owners of local property threatened legal action because the cesspools were overflowing into nearby houses.

The governors met frequently at the house in Prescot St., and later in the hospital in Whitechapel a quarterly meeting of the Court of Governers was established which all governors might attend. Seven governors were elected to form a small House Committee to meet weekly and be responsible for the hospital activities. Two of the House Committee were to go round the house twice a week to report to the Committee. This practice continued until 1948 when the NHS Act came into force.

*William Beller's* painting of the proposed new London Hospital, Whitechapel, 1752, then engraved *to raise subscriptions for the completion of the plans by Boulton Mainwaring*

The House Committee, with John Harrison as its guiding spirit, began planning a permanent building and searched for a suitable site near to a common sewer. After great difficulty, Mainwaring, the hospital surveyor and a governor, recommended a piece of ground "near the river and commonly known as the White Chapel Mount and the Mount Field". The choice was contested because "the High Road was infested with highwaymen and foot pads". Yet it proved a sound investment: the estate was large enough to allow further buildings to be developed over the years, as much of the land was purchased freehold, and the part leased from the Corporation of the City of London was held until the year 2166.

The foundation stone of the present building facing the Whitechapel Road was laid in 1752, and despite John Harrison's death a year later, the building he had envisaged was built, one floor at a time, as money became available. Five years later the first patients were admitted to part of the front block.

The early death of John Harrison at the age of 35 has been attributed to overwork and financial stress. He devoted all his energies to the development of the hospital, neglecting to maintain his private practice for his own good. In the voluntary hospital, senior medical staff were elected by the governors but they were not paid, giving their services freely until the NHS in 1948. They derived their income from private practice, and from fees charged to their pupils - the medical students.

## Patients and their treatment.

The founders in the 18th century and their successors emphasised the quality of care that was expected from all the staff. The secretary (later house governor) the matron and the apothecary (later medical officer) were required to be resident, nurses were to be "tender, diligent and compassionate to the patients, and courteous to strangers", and rules were drawn up for their conduct. Defaulters were rebuked or dismissed by the House Committee, on the recommendation of the Matron.

LONDON-INFIRMARY,
Dr. HIBBINS, Phyfician.
Wednefdays and Fridays.
The PATIENTS to attend at Eleven o'Clock.
Patient's Name.
The PATIENTS, being admitted without any Expence, are required to be conftant in their Attendance; and, when cured, to acknowledge the Benefits they have received at Chapel, and at the next Weekly Committee.
PATIENTS not complying herewith will never be admitted again; but thofe who attend their Cure, and return Thanks, will receive a Certificate thereof, which will entitle them to future Relief from this CHARITY.
1747
Chairman.

▲ *Patients Ticket of admission,*
*a recomendation by a governor, the rules for*
*attendance and thanks after cure.*

Although resources were limited, patients were offered the best accommodation that could be afforded - iron bedsteads replaced wooden ones as early as 1772, feather beds were purchased in 1820 for particular cases, and by the end of the 1870's jugs of milk were provided on each patient's bedside locker to improve their nutrition.

The early founders of The London were always struggling to make ends meet. Unlike the hospital founded by a large donation from Thomas Guy, The London Hospital despite generous donors and benefactors was never richly endowed, and always tried to do a lot with a little, and to continue the work in times of financial constraint.

From the earliest days, The London's fund raising became the focus of national and local endeavour, enjoying the support of many - from royalty to local traders and grateful patients. The London was fortunate in those who chose to serve it - as governors, treasurers, those who gave loyal service on the staff in various departments, and those who encouraged others to contribute to the financial resources needed as the hospital grew in size, and medical treatments advanced. In the 18th century the Archbishop of Canterbury was a member of the building committee - and every bishop in England encouraged financial support for the hospital. A service with a sermon in one of the city churches and a ceremonial procession followed by the Annual Feast was successful, not only in raising money but in raising public awareness of the continuing needs of "this charitable institution".

Christian motives were a strong influence in enlisting support for the voluntary hospitals and some were founded for members of the Church of England and others for different denominations.

The London from its foundation was noted for its religious tolerance. When the matron, Mrs Joanna Martin was appointed in 1757, she "was given leave to attend her own place of worship, as she was a dissenter". The first record of the appointment of chaplain to the hospital was in 1756 at £100 pa. although the incumbent Rev. Matthew Audley had been honorary chaplain since 1740 when he volunteered his services to the founders.

The practice of the ward sister saying The London Hospital Prayer in each ward at the beginning of the day continued until the middle of the 20th century. The spirit of the founders remained - a charity open to all, with respect for minority creeds and faiths which is characteristic of the hospital today.

Many benefactors were Jews, Quakers, Non -Conformists, members of other faiths and non - believers. In 1791 John Howard who had visited the Hospital in 1788 wrote to suggest that 2 wards should be set aside for Jewish patients, and the first request for separate Jewish wards came in 1816. A "Hebrew Cook" and a kosher kitchen were established in 1837. Two wards for Jewish patients were provided in 1842 after many years of local campaigning by generous donors to provide facilities for the strict dietary regime required at that time. These were the first of their kind in a British general hospital. In 1899 a gift of £10,000 repeated in 1903, for the endowment of Jewish wards, was made by Mr Edward L. Raphael and other donors including Baron N.M. de Rothschild and Mr A. Goldsmid. These wards were named Helene Raphael and Rothschild.

◄

*William Hogarth, Friend and benefactor of several other London hospitals in the eighteenth century supported The London Hospital. His drawing of the Last Judgement shows Christ gesturing towards an imaginary hospital. This drawing,in the possesion of The London, was reproduced in a series of engravings to gain publicity and support for the good work of the hospital.*

From the earliest times in Prescot St. the House Committee made it clear that some people were not to be admitted.

"no persons suspected of having
the Small Pox, itch, or any
other infections or Venereal Distemper
or judged to have a
Consumptive condition."

Arrangements were made for them to be referred to the Smallpox Hospital and at the instigation of John Harrison, a donation was made annually by the "Charity" to assist with this expense.

Treatment by the physicians for diseases - or distempers as they were known in the eighteenth century - consisted mainly of blood letting, cupping and prescribing "elixirs, decoctions, pills and potions". The drug bills were considerable -and frequently scrutinised. There were no anaesthetics for surgical operations, but in one year "£200 had been paid for malt spirit - there being 700 gallons used ".Despite wound infections and suppuration requiring frequent changes of surgical dressings, many patients recovered well, but accidents causing compound fractures accounted for a high mortality. Artificial limbs were fitted- of wood or iron - and as many amputees were treated, a gift of £100 was made to the Charity from a national fund which had been started for "the benefit of the wounded in the late rebellion" - in 1745. Children were not admitted - except

those with fractures, or requiring amputation, or for "exceptional conditions". They were mainly treated as out patients. "Persons disordered mainly in their senses" were sent to Bethlem, but those suffering from epilepsy often caused disturbances in the wards, causing some patients to relapse, or "by frightening some into the same distemper who were never subject to it before". Such patients were to be treated as out patients. It is of note that Dr. Andrée later published the first clinical report issued from "a hospital study of cases of epilepsy and allied disorders among his patients in the London Infirmary".

*Dock workers in the East End* ▲
*illustrated by Gustav Doré in the early*
*nineteenth century*

**Social conditions in the locality.**

During the first century of The London's service social conditions in the East End were appalling. Between 1801 - 1831 the population of the area almost doubled as immigration increased - refugees fleeing from wars in Europe, Jewish immigrants in Whitechapel and in

Bethnal Green, where Irish labourers settled. Poverty, inadequate fresh water supplies, lack of sanitation, poor housing, over-crowding and infestation led to outbreaks of disease - smallpox, typhus, typhoid fever, tuberculosis and cholera. These conditions, and accidents due to industries beginning to develop in the area, all added to the problems facing the hospital. The daily record of events in the hospital by the secretary, John Jenkinson in 1815 gives some glimpses of the work and the efforts made to cope with the increasing demands with limited resources - repainting and cleaning the kitchen, repairing the water closets, and trying to provide more beds for the surgeons.

"six lascars have been brought hither since Tuesday last with mortified feet - and two more are expected from the ship, ARMA - Capt. J. Read - from Bombay." Dec. 1815.

The Whitechapel Bell Foundry, established in 1420 in Houndsditch moved to the Whitechapel road in 1738. Makers of Big Ben, Bow Bell and other famous bells, also made bells for The London Hospital , a large one for the Front hall, and the operation bell, 1791

At that time hospital patients relied on sanctuary, there were very few cures for disease, and surgery was primitive until the advent of anaesthesia.

William Blizard, surgeon, philanthropist ▲ and reformer, elected to the staff in 1780.

### William Blizard and The London Hospital Medical College.

The first complete medical school in England, with systematic formal education, was established at The London in 1785. William Blizard, surgeon, was the driving force, and a physician, Thomas Maddocks was the co - founder. Two years earlier Blizard had persuaded the House Committee to allow him to give two courses of lectures on Anatomy and Surgery; but he had to bring his own patients, and his pupils were not to be allowed into the wards. One of the pupils who attended the lectures was John Abernethy, later to become the founder

*The London Hospital Whitechapel ,in the 1830's showing the Medical College on it's original site after completion of the East (1775) and West wing in 1778.*

of St. Bartholomew's Hospital Medical School. Blizard and his colleagues, mindful of the Committee's ruling that "hospital funds were subscribed solely to help the sick poor", collected resources to erect a building beside the hospital in 1783 with a lecture theatre, and facilities for teaching a full range of subjects which no other private medical college could offer at that time. This was the fore- runner of the present London Hospital Medical College built later in 1854 and extended at the turn of the century.

In 1791 Blizard's concern at seeing patients he had discharged as "cured" being readmitted within weeks because of poverty, and lack of care led to the foundation of the Samaritan Society. He led the way to assist patients with special needs for surgical appliances, or convalescence, and financed much of the work of the society in the first 4 years of its existence. Later, after a large donation from Mr. James Hora, the society was named after his wife; The Marie Celeste Samaritan

Society as it exists today.

Blizard was also responsible for selecting the quotation inscribed above the door of the Medical College which was subsequently adopted by the Hospital, and incorporated in the Nurses Badge in 1931-
Homo sum; humani nihil a me
alienum puto.

▲ *The Hospital seal, designed and made by John Ellicot F.R.S a governor and benefactor, It incorporates the idea of the Good Samaritan, and the link with the City of London.*

It is suggested by the former dean and historian, A.E. Clark Kennedy that Blizard's favourite translation of this (by Colman) was " I am a man and all human calamities come home to me ."
Alternative interpretations include that "I am human I think nothing affecting humanity is alien to me", "I am human therefore any human concern is my concern", and "no human problem is unworthy of my consideration".

Archibald Billing F.R.S ▲
elected physician 1882, a founder member of the University of London in 1817, he included regular bedside teaching - the first course of clinical teaching for medical students in England.

▲
James Maddocks, physician and co-founder with William Blizard of the London Hospital Medical College - opened October 1785

The Dental School at The London was established later in 1911, and the Dental Institute was opened in 1965. Currently The London Hospital Medical College, as a school of the University of London, provides degree courses in medicine and dentistry; collaboration between the hospital and the college continues in the teaching of medical and dental students and in post- graduate research and teaching for doctors and dentists.

The achievements of the founders, governors and members of the House Committee in the first century were outstanding. The original house in Featherstone St. in 1740, and the houses in Prescot St., were replaced by the new purpose built hospital in the Whitechapel Road in 1757 - to accommodate one hundred and sixty one patients and to treat outpatients.

By 1838 there were two hundred and forty beds, and a special Receiving Room to treat urgent accident cases. The Annual Feast or festival first held in 1742, and various other fund raising activities not only paid for these buildings, but also for the care and treatment of patients without charge.

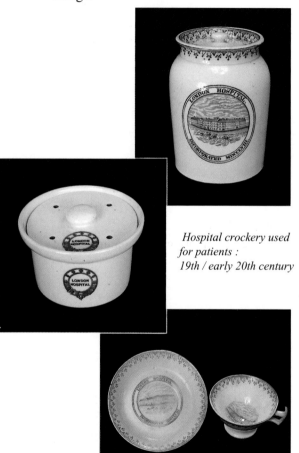

*Hospital crockery used for patients :
19th / early 20th century*

The House Committee were far sighted, setting up "a capital fund" in 1743 in anticipation of emergencies, appointing a steward a year later "to manage with due economy", and purchasing the lease of the estate from the City of London in 1745 to allow for expansion.

The Committee was, however, faced with increasing difficulties - eg, the abuse of the system of admission by "governor's letter", and the blocking of beds by the extended length of stay of some patients. In 1755 a rule was instituted that no patient should remain in the Hospital for longer than two months - a careful check on the effect of the rule was made by the Matron for the House Governor into the 1970's. There was great difficulty in attracting sufficient funds for the daily work - in 1767 the cost per bed was estimated at seventeen pounds fifteen shillings per annum - and in 1785 due to great shortage of cash, 6 wards were closed and the matron, nurses and servants discharged for a short period. By 1785 to cope with pressure of the increasing work, 3 surgeons and 3 assistant surgeons were elected. There were a similar number of physicians, and by 1827 three assistant physicians were elected. The West Wing was extended to twice its length by 1830 to increase the number of beds. Similar extension to the East Wing followed in 1840 - and in November 1840 a highly successful Anniversary Festival raised over £10,900.

As Clark Kennedy points out, during The London Hospital's first century, the nature of the work and the broad outline of medical treatment continued relatively unaltered. It was the scale of the clinical work which increased - dependent upon the funds available to provide beds for in-patients, to treat others as outpatients and to provide staff to care for them. The next 150 years were to see the growth of medical specialisation and education outstripping resources.

# CHAPTER 2

# The Voluntary Hospital - 1840 - 1948

### Scientific advances.

The Hospital's second century was one of constant change and considerable growth. Scientific discoveries, industrialisation, wars, changes in the structure of society, and an extending empire in the late Victorian era, had profound effects on the work of the hospital, and the resources available to support it. Advances in scientific knowledge gradually transformed the practice of medicine, bringing great changes in the care of patients. Increased resources were essential, not only for costly scientific equipment and for buildings to house the new departments as they evolved, but also resources to prepare the staff to meet these needs. According to the records, "the Thermometre" was first purchased at The London in 1791, and the first use of the microscope was in 1849, when it was kept in the care of the apothecary, whose title changed in 1854 to resident medical officer. The vaccination department was opened in 1860 to provide innoculation against smallpox, but other contagious diseases eg, scarlet fever and diphtheria continued to spread rapidly in the locality.

Patients with fevers or contagious diseases were left to the care of the workhouses under the Poor Law Board (1847). It was not until about 1865 that workhouse infirmaries for the sick poor began to be built in the East End to take over the care of the chronic sick and the elderly, eg, Bethnal Green, Mile End, Shoreditch, Bow and St. George's in the East.
The London Hospital, in common with other voluntary hospitals, was left with the burden of caring for acutely ill general patients, emergencies and accidents, although some patients continued to be referred by the governors. The pressure for admissions rose annually. To cope with increasing work the foundation stone of a new west wing was laid by the Prince of Wales in 1864, to be named after Princess Alexandra. A royal opening by the Duke of Cambridge was planned, but the building was opened hastily in July 1866 to allow for the admission of cholera patients.

*The first photo taken in the hospital - 1864 after Princess Alexandra's visit*

## The 1866 cholera epidemic.

Outbreaks of cholera began in England in the early 1800's. The first reports of this disease, hitherto known only to doctors who had worked in India or Asia, occurred in Sunderland. The House Committee agreed that Dr. Frederick Cobb, a physician and a clinical clerk, John Little, should have leave to investigate this. They left on January 5 th.1832, and returned three days later with the advice that if the epidemic reached the metropolis no patient with this virulent disease should be admitted to the Hospital.

In 1834 the House Committee installed a filtering system to filter all the water used in the Hospital to prevent water - borne disease. Later, in the 1850's, the water companies were obliged by law to filter water, but seepage from the river Lea contaminated the East London Water Company supplies. The great cholera epidemic of 1866 was largely confined to the East End. This brought about a change in the policy for admission in response to great need in the surrounding community. Wards in the new wing had to be opened hastily. Between July and November 1866, 858 patients were admitted with cholera and 279 with choleraic diarrhoea of whom 327 died. At the same period 12,933 were treated as out-patients. The demands on doctors and nurses were so great that the matron, Mrs. Jane Nelson, sought help from religious nursing sisters - both Anglican and Catholic, and from ladies volunteering their services, including Mrs. Catherine Gladstone the wife of William Gladstone, who became Liberal prime minister two years later. William Nixon, house governor, in an account written at the time describes the pressure of work in coping with very ill and dying patients and the measures taken to prevent the spread of the disease. Sawdust steeped in carbolic was spread about and under every bed. Sacks of straw replaced mattresses which were carried away and burnt "at the back of the hospital where we had a bonfire each night. Pickfords van came early every morning to remove the coffins of the dead".

When the epidemic ended, and the Alexandra Wing was in full use, there were 500 beds in the hospital. The pressure for admissions continued to rise despite this. During the year 1867,over 2,000 accident and 1,000 acute emergency patients were admitted, and in 1872 total admissions were 5,400.It was during the 1866 epidemic that Thomas John BARNARDO came to the Medical College planning to become a medical missionary in China. He was touched by the plight of the East End's homeless Children and dedicated the rest of his life to their welfare.

In 1873 the governors, concerned about their obligations to the local community as defined by the founders, launched an appeal for £10,000 to supplement the running costs of the hospital, and to extend the hospital to the east. They calculated a need for 800 beds. There was an immediate public response - a large sum was subscribed by the Stock Exchange, and the Grocers' Company gave £20,000. The Grocers' Wing at the east side of the hospital was opened in 1876 by Queen Victoria, whose progress through the East End was greeted with enthusiasm after her long period of mourning.

## Services for women and children.

### Midwifery.

The needs of the local community always formed part of the service offered by the Hospital. In the hospital's first century pregnant women were not admitted, although they were advised by an obstetrician. Henry Ramsbotham who had been on the staff of the medical college since 1845, was elected by the governors in 1853, and a year later "the outside maternity department" was set up to deliver women in their own homes. The "White Charity" provided for deliveries by medical students in the home, who called in the resident accoucheur when difficulties arose - bringing the mother back to hospital in a cab if necessary.

HER BEST TITLE—"QUEEN OF THE EAST."

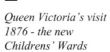

*Queen Victoria's visit 1876 - the new Childrens' Wards*

*The Receiving room 1876* ▲

*The Green Charity - midwives, the friends of the mother and baby 1914.*

*Mothers and babies on the balcony before leaving the ward to return to their dreadful housing conditions - with many families sharing one room. 1914.*

It was not until the end of the century that midwives - nurses with special experience-were employed to care for women in childbirth. Dame Rosalind Paget, who trained as a nurse at The London and who was a founder member of the National Institute of Midwifery, worked tirelessly for recognition of their expertise, which culminated in the certification of midwives in 1902.

The "Green Charity" was endowed by the benefactor, James Hora, and the Marie Celeste Maternity Department was named after his wife. The "Green Nurses" who were experienced midwives gradually took over the work from the White Charity and the medical students between 1902 and the 1920's. The London had a flourishing midwifery school from that time onwards which, in 1990, formed part of The Princess Alexandra and Newham College of Nursing and Midwifery, which three years later merged with St.Bartholomew's College of Nursing and Midwifery.

## Children.

Alexandra, Princess of Wales on her first visit to the hospital in 1864, opened the first official children's wards, and a sub - ward for maternity patients who had to be admitted.Those children's wards were amongst the first to be opened in a general hospital. Twelve years later, when HM Queen Victoria opened the Grocer's Wing, this important event set the seal on the relationship between the royal family and The London.

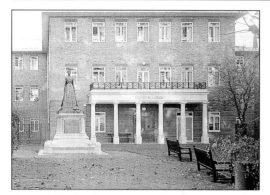

*View of The Garden House, and Queen Alexandra's statue 1990* ▲

In June 1990, HM Queen Elizabeth II unveiled a plaque to commemorate the building of the new children's unit, The Garden House. This was opened in 1991 by the Duke of Westminster, and provides clinical facilities for intensive care of the newly born, for the diagnosis and treatment of acutely ill children as in-patients and out-patients, together with overnight accommodation for parents, and teaching areas for the children, their relatives, and the staff caring for the children.

## Developing the Nursing Service.

The nursing service at The London developed from the 19th century when standards of nursing practice were set which were to influence future generations both nationally and internationally. The care of the patient as an individual provided a firm basis for all staff to contribute to their total needs. Mrs Jane Nelson, matron 1833-1867, was responsible for nursing, domestic and laundry staff and services, at a time of rapid expansion in services and new building. Miss A.M. Swift, her assistant from 1862 and matron 1867-1880, prepared the House Committee for the forthcoming changes in

nurse training, and in the welfare and care of staff, which were introduced by her successor, Miss Eva Lückes.

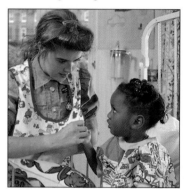

▲

*Staff Nurse and child Garden House 1993*

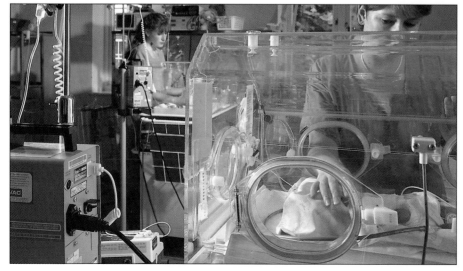

▲ *Neonatal intensive care in The Garden House 1993*

*▲ Eva Lückes, and her four assistant matrons -1911.*
*Miss Monk (1919) Miss Littleboy (1931) were her successors as matron,*

educated woman, by the standards of that time, she established the principle that "patients come first" for everyone (not only. nursing staff) who worked in the hospital, and emphasised individual responsibility, economy and accountability. Miss Lückes wrote nursing textbooks, gave lectures to nurses, arranged for them to attend lectures by physicians and surgeons, and opened the first Preliminary Training School for nurses in England in 1895 in a house given by Lord Tredegar. Her system of records for probationers and trained nurses continued until the end of World War 11. In 1885 she established the Private Nursing Institution, a separate staff of nurses to nurse patients in their own homes. Their patients included royalty, the wealthy, and also those whose fees were paid by others and by charities. The private staff nurses provided extra help in the wards between their "cases", in times of need eg, during the influenza epidemics which occurred during and after World War 1. The Private Nursing Institution which had brought international renown to The London was discontinued with the coming of the NHS. in 1948.

Miss Lückes, who had been a night sister under Miss Swift in 1879, was appointed Matron in 1880 at the age of twenty six, and for almost forty years she served The London until her death in 1919. A well

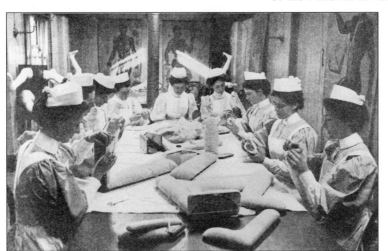

◄

*Tredegar House - the preliminary training school - the first in England opened in 1895 in the house given by Lord Tredegar.*

▲ *Miss Lückes with the 6 sisters leaving for South Africa in 1901 at the request of the Princess of Wales. 20 more sisters were sent out a year later. Several were awarded the Royal Red Cross, and some died of enteric fever.*

A fierce opponent of the movement for state registration for nurses, Miss Lückes believed in the importance of the Nurse Training School as a means of certifying proficiency in nursing. She maintained her own register of L.H. nurses - those holding appointments on the staff and elsewhere in Great Britain or in the world. Six sisters were sent to care for the wounded in the war in South Africa in 1901 at the express wish of the Princess of Wales, others joined a surgical team led by Sir Frederick Treves. Many London Hospital Nurses became matrons in the armed forces, the Colonial Nursing Service, and the mission field. Miss Annie McIntosh, Miss Luckes' assistant matron, became the matron of St. Bartholomew's Hospital in 1911.

*Miss Annie M^C Intosh, assistant matron, became Matron, St Bartholomew's Hospital. 1911.* ▲

*Sir Frederick Treves, surgeon, anatomist and teacher. He befriended the deformed and destitute Joseph Merrick, and wrote an account of the Elephant Man. He took a surgical team, including two London Hospital Sisters to South Africa in 1900 and wrote of his experiences. In 1902 he operated on King Edward VII for appendicitis.*

▶

Miss Lückes also prepared some sisters for specialised work as midwives, masseuses, and experts in nutrition and invalid cookery, thus anticipating the paramedical staff training which developed in the mid -twentieth century.

▲  *London Hospital Massage Dept, c. 1910*

Sisters who specialised in massage and exercises were responsible for teaching these arts to staff nurses from the hospital, and from elsewhere.

*Dame Rosalind Paget*  ▲

Dame Rosalind Paget who was also a trained masseuse, played a prominent part in the recognition of this work by the establishment of The Incorporated Society of Trained Masseuses, later Massage and Medical Gymnasts Society, which, in 1943 became The Chartered Society of Physiotherapy.  The first school of physio-therapy began later at The London in 1936. Sited in the Department of Physical Medicine, the school continued to provide this service until physiotherapy was established as a discipline in higher education in 1981, as The London Hospital School of Physiotherapy, University of East London.

▲  *Sydney Holland, 2nd Viscount Knutsford*

### Sydney Holland, - Viscount Knutsford.

Three remarkable people served The London from the end of the 19th. century, - Sydney Holland  (later 2nd Viscount Knutsford) who had been Chairman of Poplar Hospital, and a governor of The London, was elected to the House Committee in 1895  after discussing this with Miss Lückes. The London was fortunate

*Out Patients Department.*
*c. 1905 - 1910*

*Operating Theatre - opened 1902* ▼

that this energetic reformer and gifted fund raiser agreed to become chairman in the following year - an office he held for over 30 years - and he and Miss Lückes worked together assisted by Ernest Morris, house governor, until her death in 1919. When he was elected to the House Committee, Knutsford was appalled by the state of the vast institution. His recommendations to the House Committee to address these issues by renovation, were accompanied by the proposal to raise the original Mainwaring building by 2 floors including a laboratory, rooms to isolate patients with infected wounds and to build a new outpatient building. Alfred Yarrow, a shipping magnate gave £25,000 for the Out Patient Department. Mr. J. A. Fielden - who had been operated on by Sir Frederick Treves, gave £22,000 for the isolation block, Fielden House, later to become the Private Wards. Fielden gave £84,000 during his lifetime to support the Hospital, and bequeathed £100,000 for an endowment. The Bernhard Baron Department of Pathology was built in 1901-

financed by generous donors. It was rebuilt in 1927, and the Research Laboratories in Ashfield Street were opened in 1957. The present Institute of Pathology was built in 1965 on the site of the former Nurses' Garden, next to the Swimming Bath given to the nursing staff by Edward Meyerstein in 1935, the year of King George V's jubilee. Lord Knutsford's fund raising efforts earned him the title Prince of Beggars; he made powerful speeches, devised new Quinquennial Appeals, made an appeal on B.B.C. Radio and devised new kinds of collecting boxes, thus keeping The London Hospital in the public eye. A friend of the royal family he encouraged the Prince of Wales later King Edward VIIth to continue the interest shown in the hospital by Queen Victoria.

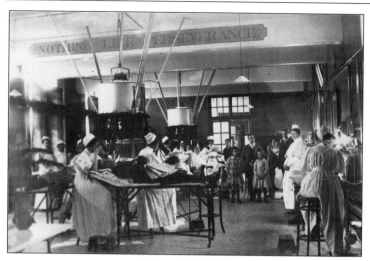

▲ *The Finsen Light Department c. 1905*

*Queen Alexandra's statue.erected by friends of the Hospital 1907*
▶

(tuberculosis of the skin). She arranged for 2 doctors and 2 nursing sisters to visit Copenhagen to learn the use of the ultraviolet technique. Many patients came from far and wide for this treatment as outpatients at The London - often given board and lodging in nearby houses by the Samaritan Society for the duration of their treatment. Although the treatment was often prolonged, its use was successful in more than 80% of patients - halting the destruction of the nose and cheeks which otherwise caused great facial disfigurement. In 1925, Sunbaths for these patients were opened with gifts from grateful patients of the Finsen treatment.

**Research and treatment.**

Research into the causes, progress and treatment of disease has always formed a major part of the work of a teaching hospital. Pioneering work was carried out by physicians and surgeons at The London from its foundation, accelerating towards the end of the 19th and early 20th centuries. This included neurology and neurosurgery, cardiology - eg, Henry Souttar's open heart surgery to stretch the mitral valve in 1925, - gastro enterology and surgery of the alimentary tract, and thoracic surgery. Studies in pathology, pharmacology, biochemistry, microbiology and radiology and other sciences opened up more complex forms of treatment for patients. This called for an investment of resources - on an ever increasing scale.

The King, accompanied by Queen Alexandra, opened the Out-Patients Department in 1903, two years after his operation by Sir Frederick Treves which took place two days before the date fixed for the coronation. Queen Alexandra became President in 1904 and took an active interest in the hospital until her death in 1925. As a Danish princess, one of her many gifts in 1899 was the Finsen Light treatment which she caused to be brought from Denmark for treating lupus vulgaris

Lord Knutsford found the money for countless improvements, as research opened new avenues of treatment.

▲  *X Ray Diagnosis 1896*

The year 1995 marks the centenary of the discovery of X-rays - first used for diagnosis at The London the following year in 1896. The first radium was purchased almost fifteen years later. In 1935 a gramme of radium was given to the Hospital by the Medical Research Council to produce the gas, radon, for use in seeds for clinical use in some forms of cancer. The Department of Radiotherapy, established in 1943 serves as an example of progress in scientific knowledge and the increasing complexity of treatment which ensues. Between 1958 -1973 the department was rebuilt, from a room in the basement of the Front Block of the Hospital, to include the equipment required to meet these advances, and the specialist staff to use the sophisticated machines. At that time the title was changed to Radiotherapy and Oncology Department to indicate the clinical nature of the work - radiation therapy, hormonal and chemotherapy. In 1985 this department was altered. The C T scanner in Neuro Xray and the compatible therapy planning system were installed in 1985 to augment the existing equipment, and the Sir Maxwell Joseph Chair of Medical Oncology was established. At the present time there are 2 Linear Accelerators, and 1 being installed, 1 Cobalt Unit, 1 superficial unit and contact unit, 1 orthovoltage unit, 1 simulator and 1 treatment planning computer. A micros-electron is being commissioned. Today The Royal London Hospital treats patients, and offers doctors, nurses and radiographers both teaching and experience in highly specialised treatment and in palliative radiotherapy, and provides opportunities for post graduate research. The Radiography School developed as part of the department of radiography and radiotherapy. It opened in 1946 with 14 students, and a small self-contained classroom in the attics of the

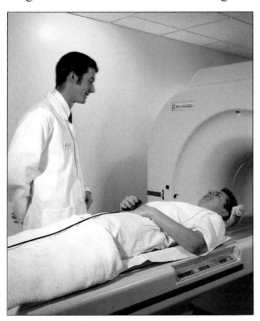

▲  *M R I Scanner 1994*

*Wounded ▶*
*First World War*

WOUNDED SOLDIERS KING EDWARD WARD LONDON HOSPITAL 2

▲ *Laboratory investigations. 1933*

Lückes Home. Fourteen students were admitted annually, and there were over 300 applicants for the first course in 1946. In the early 1990's the Radiography School combined with several other regional schools to form an academic centre at Charterhouse College of Radiography. Clinical experience for students is provided at several sites, including The Royal London Hospital.

### The Hospital in wartime.

Two world wars brought lasting effects calling for increased resources. The Hospital suffered from bombing in both. Almost twenty times between 1914 and 1918 bombs fell on the East End, and the basement corridors of the hospital were used as air raid shelters.

### World War 1.

During World War 1, when many doctors and nurses were called to service in the armed forces, shortages of medical staff led to some American and women doctors being employed. Between 1918 and 1922 women medical students were accepted by the medical college because of reduced wartime intakes of students and war casualties. Women students were not accepted again until 1946! Dorothy Russell, who joined the staff in the early 1920's to work with Professor Turnbull in the Pathology Department, became one of the first women to hold a medical chair in 1947, when she succeeded him as Professor of Morbid Anatomy.

In addition to pressures of work caused by staff shortages, the Hospital "housed" Belgian refugees and soldiers driven from their country by the German invasion. The first British wounded soldiers were received at the request of the War Office on Sunday August 30th 1914

less than 4 weeks after the outbreak of war, being transported from the docks in vans provided by J.Lyons & Co., as there was a shortage of ambulances at that time. One hundred were admitted on that day, and two hundred on the next day. During the whole of World War 1 - 6,533 wounded were admitted to the hospital. A ward was set aside for wounded officers, and Sir John Lavery R.A. came from Dublin to record his impressions of treatment, and gave the copyright of his oil paintings to the Hospital.

In June 1917 at 11 am. bombs fell near Aldgate - 207 injured were brought to the Hospital, 75 were admitted, 44 of whom died and 30 were brought in dead. Night raids replaced day time bombing, and the local people crowded into the hospital to take shelter believing they would be safe. In January 1918 4 tons of T.N.T. were blown up at the munition works at Silvertown - devastating a square mile of houses, breaking the Hospital windows. Shortages of drugs, bandages and dressings called for great economy in the use of supplies. Miss Beatrice Monk, Assistant Matron, became Steward of the hospital, and five years later, on the death of Miss Lückes, succeeded her as Matron. The costs incurred during the war and the debts that had accumulated added to the problems facing Lord Knutsford, and the House Committee. The influenza epidemic in 1918 / 19 was more virulent than any previous outbreaks. Patients died quickly from broncho-pneumonia. Wards were set aside for such patients who with the staff caring for them had extra rations, and the nurses were required to wear face masks.

There was a high mortality in December 1918, 96 died out of 146 admitted. In February 1919, 3 nurses and 80 patients died. In the late 1950's a similar virulent outbreak of influenza occurred, affecting mainly the younger members of the Hospital staff. Gloucester Ward was reserved for their care, but a young student nurse died of pneumonia.

It was also clear as World War 1 drew to its close, that The London was changing with the social upheaval of the times. The costs escalated and the price of commodities rose dramatically; in the post war years of depression and high taxation there were diminishing voluntary contributions. Staff recruitment, particularly the recruitment of women and entrants to nurse training, became difficult because of the changes in the role of women in wartime, and alternative opportunities in other professions. The system of nurse training continued until State Registration was first introduced in 1925. Miss Monk, in order to assist recruitment, introduced the three year training course followed by one year as a staff nurse for The London Hospital School of Nursing Certificate.

*The London Hospital Badge - instituted* ▲ *by Miss Monk in 1931 - and from 1943 presented by the Board of Governors, ( later the Special Trustees ) to all nurses who completed training and passed the Final State Examination*

The " Appeals Thermometer " on the front of the hospital above the entrance showed the amount of money needed daily to keep the Hospital open, and recorded the amount by which expenditure outstripped resources. Despite long waiting lists for admission and severe epidemics some wards had to be closed for a year. Two successful Quinquennial Appeals assisted with maintenance, and an anonymous donor gave over £171,000 for endowment.

*Viscount Knutsford and Queen Alexandra on her last visit as President July 1921* ▲

Advances in surgical treatment and anaesthesia, in medicine and pharmacology added to the cost of patient care. The use of insulin for diabetes in 1923 and the discovery of liver extract to treat pernicious anaemia added to drug costs. The latter was estimated to cost £1 per day for each patient. The problems of increased running costs were accompanied by the need for refurbishment after World War 1, and anxieties caused by the vulnerability of the Hospital to air attack. In 1931, Lord Knutsford died in the hospital he had loved and worked for and Sir William Goschen succeeded him as chairman, an office he held until his death in 1943.

## World War 11.

World War 11 was to have a profound effect on nursing and medical care. So, too was the advent of chemotherapy - the sulphonamide drugs discovered in 1933, the anti tubercular drugs, penicillin in 1943 and streptomycin in 1946, and the other antibiotics which developed later and radically altered the patients' treatment.

▲   *Evacuation children taken to safety - 1940*

Before the outbreak of the World War 11 the Ministry of Health arranged an Emergency Medical Service. Russell Howard senior consultant general surgeon at The London was appointed by the Ministry of Health to advise on the co-ordination of work in all the hospitals - both voluntary and municipal in Sectors 1 and 11 - East and North East London, the whole of Essex and parts of Middlesex and Hertfordshire, and to advise on the recruitment of honorary staff into a salaried Emergency Medical Service.

On September 2nd. 1939 many of The London's staff and patients were evacuated to emergency hospitals in these Sectors - whilst emergency beds on the ground and first floors were available in

▲ *Wartime at The London Hospital Annexe Brentwood .Smoking was not regarded as a health hazard in 1941.*

Whitechapel.  Staff were later withdrawn from some of these units in 1941 when The London Hospital Annexe at Brentwood opened.  The Annexe, a hutted hospital, provided 345 beds for general medical and specialised surgical treatment - neurosurgery, gynaecology, and thoracic surgery.  An additional 70 beds were provided for patients with tuberculosis. The chairman, Sir William Goschen, and his successor in 1943, Sir John Mann, the house governor Henry Brierley, the acting matron Alice Burgess and her assistants worked tirelessly to maintain outpatient and in-patient services to the surrounding district, and to work with A.E. Clark Kennedy the dean of the medical college and the senior sister tutor Annie Harris to continue the education of medical and nursing students.The Receiving Room (as the Accident and Orthopoedic Department was known at that time) the Outpatient Department, and the midwifery and dental services continued

▲   *Professor Turnbull views the damage to the post mortem room - August 1944.*

▼   *200th Anniversary visit of King and Queen - 1940*

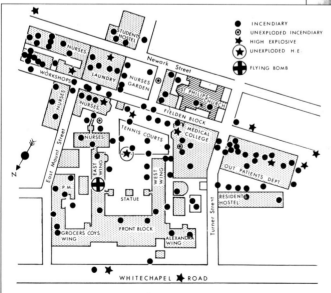

INCENDIARY
UNEXPLODED INCENDIARY
HIGH EXPLOSIVE
UNEXPLODED H.E.
FLYING BOMB

their work throughout the war in response to local needs.  During the Blitz, which in London was directed at the East End, The London was bombed by high explosives in 1941 and 1942, causing damage to the laundry, part of the Alexandra and Lückes Nurses Homes, the Outpatients' Department and the Medical College.  On the night of 3rd/4th August 1944 a flying bomb

*Bombs on the Hospital World War II*  ▲

◀ *Midwifery services continued despite the Blitz, Miss Dear setting out on a home visit in Whitechapel.*

## Professions Allied To Medicine.

War also brought to light the need for a team approach in the treatment of the sick and injured, and gave further impetus to the provision of experience and teaching for students in the professions allied to medicine,and those providing technical and support services. The London was foremost in providing nutritional advice. The children's department was established in 1926 by Sir Robert Hutchison, who had earlier advised the House Committee on the need to improve the diet in the Hospital. Miss Rose Simmonds a Sister Dietician was one of the first nurses to obtain a Rockefeller scholarship to study in North America in 1926. Twenty years later, Ella Scott, Sister Dietician also studied in the United States with a grant from the same foundation, and on her return plans were made for post graduate students to gain experience in the wards and the Department for 6 months to qualify as clinical dieticians and to gain recognition by the British Dietetic Association. In 1949, an Occupational Therapy Department was opened in a room in the Department of Physical Medicine, and the students gained experience in preparation for qualification of the College of Occupational Therapists. Later in 1989 a post graduate diploma in occupational therapy for students holding a first degree was established at Queen Mary and Westfield College, jointly accredited and validated, by the College of Occupational Therapists and The London Hospital Medical College on behalf of the University of London.

killed two patients and injured two nurses as it destroyed part of the East Wing.

Throughout the war, staff in all departments maintained the essential services on which the hospital depended - domestic, the linen room, catering, laundry, portering, the works department, laboratory, pharmacy, telephone and clerical staff. Fire spotters, emergency first aid workers and messengers were recruited from off duty staff and local residents. At the end of the war, medical and nursing staff and others were withdrawn from the sector hospitals as wards began to be re-opened slowly at The London.

World War II increased the need for social support for many patients and their families. The pre-war role of the lady almoner first appointed in 1909 was replaced by a department of social work established in 1943, with two social workers in the hospital to liaise with local authorities and voluntary agencies.

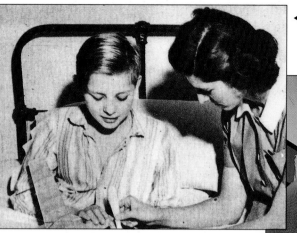

◄ *Therapists -*
*Occupational therapy. 1949*

▼ *Therapists -Physiotherapy, 1993*

Research and treatment carried out during the war also led to further developments in microbiology and pharmacy, and in 1947 the first training courses for laboratory technicians within the educational sector were established in the Institute of Pathology at The London jointly with Sir John Cass College, leading to recognition by the Medical Laboratory Technicians' Board for the Council of Professions Allied to Medicine. From the mid-1970's these diploma courses, and the degree courses which developed later, were validated for the Institute of Medical Laboratory Scientists.

In September 1958, a one year course for dental chairside assistants began. Six students were admitted twice each year - later altered to 12 annually - and they were expected to remain for six months on the staff on completion of the course, to receive recognition and a badge. Currently the Dental School prepares 8 students annually as Dental Therapists/ Hygienists for recognition by the General Dental Council, undertakes research projects into the scientific basis of dental health, and participates in the development of oral health promotion and education carried out by a team established by the Tower Hamlets Family Health Service.

◄ *Research Laboratory. 1993*

Students of these and other disciplines continue to gain experience under supervision to maintain services which are essential to patient care, eg, speech therapy, audiology, chiropody, clinical psychology. Staff and students are also offered teaching in safety at work, lifting, and first aid.

▲ *Clare Alexander, Matron interviewing Helen Marshall.*

## Nursing Education.

Miss Clare Alexander, who returned to The London as matron in 1941 introduced changes in nursing education. In 1946 the training course was reduced from 4 to 3 years, and each nurse completing the course and gaining state registration, was presented with a certificate and The London Hospital badge by the Board of Governors. In the early 1950's a combined course was instituted for student nurses from The Mildmay Mission Hospital, Shoreditch, a Christian hospital founded in the 1850's as a result of the work of the Rev. William Pennefather. Later in the 1980's Mildmay became a centre for the care and treatment of people suffering from AIDS.

In 1967, with the help of generous donors, the purpose built college which bears her name was opened by Princess Alexandra. From that date, experimental courses in general and mental nursing, and courses for registration and a University of London degree in social science or economics were offered. In the 1970's other nursing schools in nearby hospitals were amalgamated with the Princess Alexandra School - Mile End, St. Clements, Bethnal Green, and the London Jewish Hospitals. This College building also allowed post registration courses in specialised nursing

▲ *Opening the Princess Alexandra School of nursing 1967. HRH. Princess Alexandra, Sir Giles Guthrie, Governor and Benefactor, Matron, Miss P Friend, John Scarlett, House Governor and the Principal, Miss S. M. Collins.*

to be developed to support scientific, medical and technological advances in clinical practice eg, intensive therapy, sexually transmitted disease, renal and neurological nursing.

*The Works Outing for craftsmen and apprentices to the Cheddar Gorge. c. 1935*

▶

## Amenities for patients and staff.

Throughout its long history, The London Hospital demonstrated its concern for the welfare of all the staff on whom the standard of patient care depends. Pension schemes for nurses, treatment for all staff during illness, and gratuities for long serving members of hospital staff were established in the late eighteenth century long before the coming of state support by national insurance, social security and the NHS. In addition to the assistance given to patients by the Marie Celeste Samaritan Society, amenities for patients such as, overnight accommodation and meals for relatives of the seriously ill, telephone trolleys for the wards, and the trolley shop were established prior to the NHS. The Social Society grew out of the Nurses' Sports and Swimming Club in 1949, and the salary of a social secretary was met from "free funds". A library for staff and patients, tennis courts, the garden and swimming pool were also supported from these sources.

## The Hospital Chapel.

The original chapel in the Mainwaring building was very large but during the renovation in 1890 it was closed to allow for some expansion on the upper floors. St. Philips' Church, Stepney Way had opened in that same year as the Hospital church. The architect therefore incorporated a smaller chapel in his design for the front entrance. As this chapel was not readily accessible, in the late 1960's in response to increasing pressure for change, The Christian Centre in the basement of the Alexandra Home was opened. This provided an ecumenical centre, a chapel, small meeting room and a chaplain's room. Services for all Christian denominations were arranged. The Centre was opened in 1967 by the Bishop of Stepney, the Moderator of the Free Church, and the Cardinal Archbishop of Westminister. Amongst the gifts for the centre was a tapestry depicting the Last Supper. In 1989, as part of the development of the

# SCANNING FACE OF A FINER LONDON YET TO BE

Grocers' Wing funded by the Special Trustees, the present chapel was opened on the ground floor in the centre of the Hospital, thus offering easy access for patients, relatives and friends, as well as staff. The Chaplaincy includes Anglican, Roman Catholic, Methodist and Free Church chaplains, the Jewish Rabbi, the Imam and other visiting clergy.

*Plans for Post War development. 1946* ▲
*(The London County Council model*
*for developement in the East End.)*

# CHAPTER 3

# The London Hospital in the NHS.

### Post - war development.

Wartime experience of working with hospitals in the sectors, with the injection of Exchequer monies to maintain essential services, had highlighted the need for strategic planning in the provision of hospital services. When the war ended in addition to other social reforms it became national policy to provide a health service for the whole population. In 1946 the Act of Parliament was passed, and from the appointed day July 5th 1948 the state accepted responsibilty for the financial future of voluntary hospitals, which were nationalised, and ceased to be the property of their boards of governors. Treasury funds for the NHS were to be raised by taxation, by levies on local authorities and from individuals' and employers' national insurance contributions. At the same time hospitals under the control of the local

by county councils, eg, Mile End, Bethnal Green, and St. Clements under LCC control. Fourteen Regional Hospital Boards were established in England to supervise the administration and medical policy of the hospitals within each region, but the teaching hospitals ( hospitals responsible for medical education and research ) were exempt from this policy and their boards were directly accountable to the Ministry of Health. Boards of governors were extended and broadened to include repesentatives of the public and professional interests. Sir John Mann remained as chairman of The London Hospital Board of Governors until 1960 when Mr. Henry R. Moore became chairman until 1974, when he became chairman of the North East Thames Regional Health Authority.

*Sir John Mann with HM.Queen Mary, views his portrait by James Gunn - a gift from the nursing staff 1949*

▶

authorities, providing acute and long term care for general and mentally ill patients were also transferred to the NHS under control of Regional Hospital Boards. Such hospitals, originally institutions under the Poor Law Board, had been further developed

### Free Funds and the Special Trustees.

On the introduction of the NHS in July 1948, The London, in common with other voluntary hospitals, retained the endowment funds to provide additional amenities for

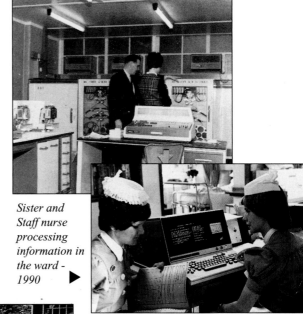

*The information revolution - ▶*
*Michael Fairey in 1964,*
*the National Elliott 803 digital computer,*
*now in the Science Museum.*

patients and staff. These monies which
were derived from legacies and donations,
carefully invested over the years, became
"free funds" under the control of the Board
of Governors. The staff accommodation in
Knutsford House and John Harrison House
are examples of the use to which these funds
contributed. On the introduction of the NHS
Reorganisation Act in 1974, these funds
were transferred to the "Special Trustees"
who are responsible for their use, under
the Charities' Act.

*Sister and*
*Staff nurse*
*processing*
*information in*
*the ward -*
*1990* ▶

▲   *Fundraising - The Street Fair 1993.*

### The Friends of The Royal London Hospital.

The Friends of The London Hospital, an
association under the patronage of
Princess Margaret, was set up in 1979 to
assist with raising funds to be made readily
available for smaller projects to improve
the comfort of patients, which could not
be met from exchequer funds, eg, curtains
and furnishings and other equipment.
Their work has continued to support the
Trust, and membership

includes former patients,
members of staff, benefactors
and local people.  East Enders
continue to support the Friends
and look upon the Hospital as
their own, which they and their
forbears supported by voluntary donations.

In the post-war world,
The London continued to
provide and develop the service offered to
its patients. Rebuilding part of the Hospital
was inevitable due to the damage caused by
bombing - particularly in the east wing, and
the up - grading of wards was long overdue.
This was carried out in two phases between
1958-60, and in the 1970's, and then continued
piecemeal. Centralisation of supplies of
sterile equipment in 1955 provided a quicker
and safer service to wards and departments
as the length of the patients' stay in hospital
shortened, the turnover of patients
increased, and the bed occupancy rose.

## Technological advances.

The London was the first hospital to purchase its own computer in 1964 to cope with increasingly complex financial systems. By 1967 its use had been extended to many other departments in the Hospital to improve the support systems on which medical, para-medical and nursing care depend and The London was invited to join the NHS Experimental Computer Project.

The John Ellicott Computer Centre rapidly developed integrated information systems which provided better patient and staff data, and assisted scheduling. The Royal London Hospital is one of the national pilot schemes for resource management which currently provides one of the most successful health information systems in Europe, providing data for effective future planning in addition to the best use of existing resources.

Medical and scientific discoveries expanding rapidly in the 1970's from pioneering work in the 1960's and in previous decades continue to affect the patient's diagnosis and treatment. In 1917, Hurry Fenwick, consultant urologist at The

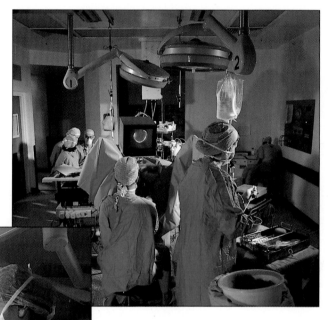

*The Laser surgery in the Kneale Jones theatres - 1993* ▲

London, was appointed the first pro-fessor of urology in the University of London. Renal transplant surgery began at The London in 1968. The first Kolff twincoil machine for renal dialysis was used in 1959. Later in 1968, The Hanbury Dialysis Unit, the first purpose built unit in the country, was established to treat patients in the Unit or in their own homes. Cardiac investigations opened new

*Day care surgery unit - 1993* ▲

*The 25th Anniversary of the Hanbury Dialysis Unit.February 1993,*

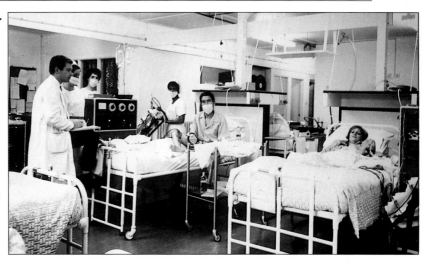

*The first pharmacy-based Drug Information Centre in London was established, and pharmacists and clinicians collaborated to produce the first complete Guide to the Prescribing of Medicines Formulary - subsequently adopted by other health authorities.*

suite on the third floor of the main block, later moved to an enlarged unit in the East Wing. Eight operating theatres, 5 of which were built in 1902, the gift of Mr. B.W. Levy at a cost of £ 13,000, and a gynaecological theatre, a gift of Mr. L. S. Bader in 1925 continued to provide for the expanding surgical services, both general and specialist surgery, until the existing theatres in the Alexandra Wing were opened by HM. The Queen in 1982.

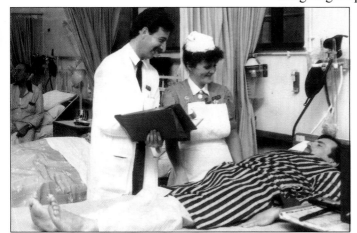

*The Hanbury Ward renal dialysis day centre 1971*

avenues of treatment, heart and lung surgery became more readily available with the advent of high technology, new surgical techniques, new forms of anaesthesia and effective control of infection. Post- anaesthetic care became more complex and a six bay unit was provided in the theatre suite in the 1950's.

The Intensive Therapy Department was opened in 1968 in the operating theatre

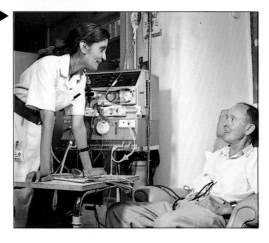

### Health and Social needs in the community.

For the first 25 years of the NHS, The London was not only called upon to provide general and specialist services as a district general hospital, but also to respond to increasing pressure for the prevention and treatment of ill health due to social conditions - as it had in the early days of its foundation. There has always been a pressing need for health care in the locality and changes in the local population, in age, size of families, in the multicultural mix in a pluralistic society, increased this need for health care in Tower Hamlets. A shortage of resident general practitioners in the locality, and the over-stretched resources of the local public health authorities made for difficulty in coping with the needs in an area of social deprivation before 1948. This continued after the NHS became responsible, and considerable demands on The London's Out -patient and Accident and Emergency services therefore continued.

In the late 1960's and early 70's discussions between representatives of the local authority and The London were established - to identify ways of closer liaison to meet these needs. The work of the General Practitioners' Liaison Committee, and the development of joint services for maternity, mental health, care of children, nursing and social work, helped to assess needs, and to try to provide care for the community based on research. The London acted as host to the Joint Hospital Services Committee for Tower Hamlets, which examined the facilities offered in the borough in ten hospitals. This experience in collaboration paved the way for an integrated district health service in East London and was the basis for the

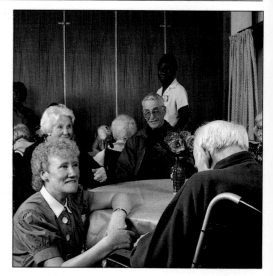

*Elderly care -*
*The Bancroft Unit, Mile End . 1993* ▲

administrative re-organisation that occurred in 1974. In 1968, in fulfilment of a long term plan first mooted in the 1940's the North East Metropolitan Regional Hospital Board and Department of Health determined that Mile End Hospital and St. Clements Hospital should become part of The London, followed by Bethnal Green in the 1974 NHS reorganisation. The London Hospital Annexe Brentwood closed in 1970. Thus The London was moving towards the principle that patients should be treated in their own locality, which underlies current government policy.

### The 1974 NHS Reorganisation Act.

Changes in the administration and control of the health and social services which were introduced in the 1974 Act, established a three tier management structure - district, area and region. Hospitals, health centres and public health activities were unified under control of the City and East London Area Health Authority. For

▲ *The Service to the community - the Hospital cares for East Enders and others whatever their creed or colour.*

managerial convenience the Area Health Authority was divided into three Districts, Newham, Tower Hamlets and City and Hackney. Within each district a Community Health Council was given the role of local representation of patients' views, to be consulted on major proposals for change. The London - with its constituent hospitals - Whitechapel, Mile End, St. Clements - together with the associated community health services comprised the Tower Hamlets District. A district management team of officers was responsible for planning this comprehensive service - by the method of concensus management. The Board of Governors along with other man-agement bodies was dissolved.

This change in managerial structure brought changes which were in many ways more profound, and were felt more keenly by staff at all levels at The London, than the transition from voluntary hospital to the NHS in 1948. As part of a larger geographically based structure - the Area - The London lost most of the control of its own affairs, and many of the functions it had built up over the years.

This large reorganisation of the NHS, with decision making subject to scrutiny by area and regional authorities, continued until 1982, against a background of social change and instability. Although strategic thinking was strengthened, day to day management of services suffered by the long chain of command and consensus management.

In 1970, government policy of reducing treasury monies from London, and the 4 metropolitan regional health authorities, in favour of other regions, reduced the monies available for the areas and districts in London. The 1970's and early 80's were difficult years in the NHS and at The London. Social unrest, leading to unprecedented industrial action in the health service, took place in many areas, during 1977-1979 and again in 1988 - 1989, presenting increased difficulties for The London. Nevertheless both the traditional and new hospital services, though reduced by financial constraints, were maintained by loyal and dedicated staff. Despite ward closures, efforts were made to support new developments, eg, in experimental joint replacement surgery and mechanics, the opening of the Bone and Joint Unit in 1977; the study of protracted pain in the Department of Therapeutics 1978 - 1982 funded by the Regional Health Authority and the Cancer Relief Fund, and the setting up of new health care projects in Steels Lane Health Centre, in the former East End Maternity Home, Commercial Road.

On the 24th March 1982, the opening of the Alexandra Wing by HM The Queen, and her warm reception by staff in all departments lightened a challenging period. The Queen toured the Emergency and Accident Department, the new sterile supply department and operating theatres, and the new academic departmental accommodation and laboratories provided by the medical college, where research is undertaken.

*H M The Queen opens Alexandra Wing 1982.* ▲

## Further NHS Changes.

The 1982 revision of the NHS removed the area health authority level and Tower Hamlets became a health authority in its own right. The London Hospital - Whitechapel, Mile End, St.Clements with the local community services provided a comprehensive range of services to the people of Tower Hamlets and beyond, throughout the years from 1982 to 1991. The concept of concensus management was replaced in 1985 by general managers with executive authority at region and district level. Tower Hamlets became one of two districts in the region to participate in management budgeting in the units. The development of day surgery, and the provision of short stay wards led to a reduction in the number of beds available for acute services. The up-grading of the main block operating theatres was completed in 1986 - to support the new Kneale Jones theatres in the Alexandra Wing. Non-invasive surgical techniques, including laser technology, investigative innovations such as gastro-intestinal endoscopy, and new fears about communicable diseases, including AIDS, were altering the basis on which treatment was costed.

## The Royal London Hospital Archives and Museum.

In 1984, an archivist was appointed through funds made available by the Special Trustees to preserve The London's historical records together with those of other hospitals and health care bodies in Tower Hamlets. Pictorial displays and exhibits and facilities for research are available in The Royal

London Hospital Archives and Museum Centre. This is a Registered Museum under the Museum and Galleries Commission, which was opened by the Lord Chancellor in November 1989 to provide a permanent home for records of health care in Tower Hamlets. This includes the extensive records of The Royal London Hospital, dating from its foundation in 1740.

*The 250th Anniversary -* ▲
*Memorabilia 1982 currently available from*
*The Royal London Hospital Shop.*

## The 250th. Anniversary - The Royal London Hospital.

The 250th Anniversary was a very special occasion because the celebrations for the 200th anniversary were cancelled on account of the outbreak of World War 11. The occasion was marked by a service in St. Paul's Cathedral, attended by many present and former staff, friends, benefactors and well wishers. The Anniversary Feast, a dinner at the Guildhall on the 12th. June 1990 was a splendid occasion based on the Annual Feast instituted by the Hospital's founder, John Harrison.

In 1990 the Ambrose King Centre, the refurbished department for sexually transmitted diseases, formerly the Whitechapel Clinic together with the Graham Hayton Centre for sufferers from HIV/AIDS, the neurosciences unit in the Alexandra Wing, and the Trauma unit were established.

The helicopter pad on the roof, and the Helicopter Emergency Medical Service opened in 1985 became fully functioning - with initial funding from the Express Newspapers. Alexandra House initially opened by Princess Alexandra in 1887 as a nurses home, was refurbished as a staff restaurant and offices in 1991, and the Lady Mayoress officially opened the Gardens provided by monies from the Inner City Development Funds and land-scaped by the gardeners of the City Corporation.

▲ *H M The Queen accompanied by Lord Knutsford visits the Accident & Emergency department 1990*

## Mergers in Medical and Nursing Education.

In 1990 plans for joint development of preclinical medical and dental education between the medical colleges at The London Hospital and St. Bartholomew's Hospital, linked with Queen Mary and Westfield College, University of London, came to fruition. In line with statutory changes in nursing education, The Princess Alexandra and Newham College of Nursing and Midwifery was formed by the merger of the two nursing and two midwifery schools in Tower Hamlets and

*The Lady Mayoress* ▲
*opens the landscaped gardens - July 1992*
*Sir William Staveley, Chairman*
*The Royal London and Associated Community*
*Services N H S Trust*

*The Helicopter Emergency Medical Service opened as part of the intergrated major trauma facilities at the Royal London in 1990* ▲

Newham Health Districts. In 1991 the College in conjunction with the University of Greenwich, was approved for the accreditation of nursing studies and the higher award of the English National Board for qualified nurses. In October 1992 the first course for registration in nursing and a university diploma in nursing studies commenced between the College and Queen Mary and Westfield, and Goldsmiths' Colleges. On April 1st. 1993 the Princess Alexandra and Newham College of Nursing and Midwifery merged with St. Bartholomew's College of Nursing and Midwifery, in line with current policy of the statutory bodies and regional health authority. From 1994 the new college - The St. Bartholomew, Princess Alexandra and Newham College of Nursing and Midwifery became linked with the City University, severing the previous associa-tion with two colleges of the University of London - Queen Mary and Westfield and Goldsmiths'.

▲ *Community Midwife 1993*

# CHAPTER 4

# The Royal London Hospital and Associated Community Services NHS Trust.

In 1989 the NHS was again in the throes of another major reform to establish the internal market in health care by creating self-governing hospitals to provide services to health authorities on the basis of contracts. The Royal London applied for self-governing status in the first wave of applications to become what is known as a National Health Service Trust. The Royal London Hospital and Associated Community Services NHS Trust (established by statutory instrument 1990 No.2438) came into effect on 21 st .December 1990 - and specified an operational date of April 1st. 1991. From that date the Trust took full management responsibility for the hospital and community health services previously held by the Tower Hamlets District Health Authority.

The strategy for the future was set out in a mission statement, and in the Annual report. The new Trust aimed to be the main providers of integrated health care in East London; to provide a high quality service responsive to all those using the facilities; to support research and development and to provide facilities for the training of medical and dental students at the London Hospital Medical College and Dental School and for the training of other health care professionals.The Trust Board consisted of a chairman, a chief executive, 4 executive members, and 5 non executive members. A quality assurance team led by the director of nursing and quality assurance, was appointed with the remit to monitor and implement change throughout the Trust on a multidisciplinary basis.

During the year to March 31st. 1993 the first stage of the site strategy was achieved by consolidating acute services at

The Royal London Hospital, Whitechapel, opening the day stay surgical unit on January 29th. 1993, and the enlarged Accident and Emergency department on February 24th. 1993. The 144 bed Bancroft Unit at Mile End offering both acute and continuing care and rehabilitation for the elderly was provided, and in January 1993 new wards dedicated to mental health services for the elderly moved from St. Clements to Mile End to integrate them fully with other continuing care services for the elderly. The second stage of the strategy, with help from the Special Trustees, and the Regional Health Authority, is in hand in 1993/94 to establish a rehabilitation unit, a rheumatology unit, a diabetic day care centre, facilities for general practitioners and community health teams at Mile End.

*The Royal London Hospital N H S Trust,.* ▲
*Chairman, Michael Haines,( Right )*
*chief executive Michael Fairey,*
*medical director, Michael Swash.*

# CHAPTER 5

# The Royal Hospitals NHS Trust.

Following publication in February 1993 of "Making London Better", the Government's response to the report on London's health services (Tomlinson 1992) and the specialty reviews which followed, the merger was proposed of The London Chest Hospital, The Royal London Hospital and The Royal Hospital of St. Bartholomew. On April 1st. 1994 The Royal London Hospital NHS Trust was dissolved, and a new Trust encompassing the merged hospitals and their services was established - called The Royal Hospital of St. Bartholomew, The Royal London Hospital and The London Chest Hospital NHS Trust ( The Royal Hospitals NHS Trust )

In the words of the new chairman Sir Derek Boorman, this merger offers these 3 hospitals the opportunity to combine their strengths and expertise in the interests and care of patients in the City and East London and beyond.

The City and East London Family and Community Health Services Agency to manage primary and community services within City and Hackney, Newham and Tower Hamlets - from April 1st. 1994 until March 1995 was also formed - with the inclusion of current services at Mile End and St. Clements. These changes are likely to have far reaching effects on the provision of an integrated health service for East Enders.

*The Royal Hospitals N H S Trust.*
*Chairman Sir Derek Boorman, with*
*Miss Pam Hibbs, Miss Alison Knapp, opening the*
*Patient advice and information centre June 1994.*
▼

# Conclusion - towards the next century.

" The London Hospital Illustrated " edited Claire Daunton published by Batsford provides a pictorial record of the 250 years of service at The Royal London Hospital. A copy was presented to H M The Queen on her visit in 1990, when she unveiled a plaque to commemorate the building of the new Children's Unit, the Garden House. At this visit when H M The Queen granted the title "Royal" to the hospital whose Royal Charter was granted in 1757, she gave her permission

" In recognition of the quality of care and the dedication to teaching and research the hospital had shown over 250 years".

The state's intervention/control since 1948 created complex administrative arrangements within the health service. The challenge for the new Trust as it moves forward to the next century will be to restore the balance between the multi- professional team caring for patients and those whose role it is to support, and provide for, their efforts to succeed.

Despite all the changes that have occurred over the years, and whatever changes occur in the governance of The Royal London Hospital in the future, the present staff and their successors inherit the spirit of service, the tradition of caring, and commitment to the local population established by the founders.

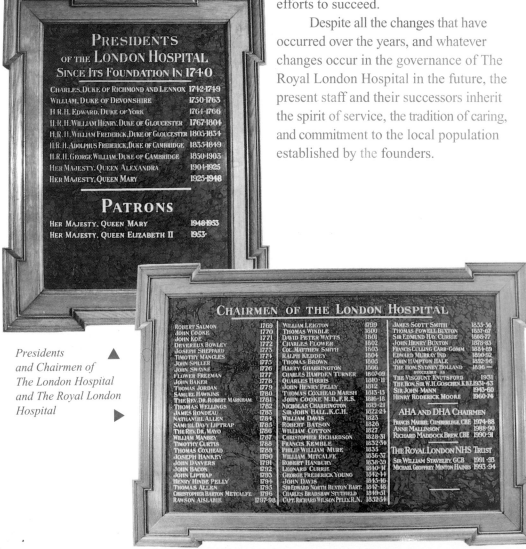

*Presents ▲
and Chairmen of
The London Hospital
and The Royal London
Hospital ▶*

# Further reading.

**Broadley M.E :**
> *Patients come first.* Pitman Medical, London 1980.

**Clark Kennedy A.E :**
> *London Pride-The Story of a Voluntary Hospital.* Hutchinson Benham.London 1979.
> *The London, A Study in the Voluntary Hospital System. Two Volumes, 1962 / 1963* Pitman London
> *Edith Cavell.Pioneer and Patriot.* Faber and Faber 1965.

**Collins S.M :**
> *Two Victorian Matrons. The London Hospital.* RCN History of Nursing Journal. 1994.

**Daunton C :**
> *The London Hospital Illustrated.* Batsford. London 1990.
> *Edith Cavell - Her Life and Her Art. Sa vie et son art.* Published RLH 1990.

**Ellis J.R :**
> *The London Hospital Medical College 1785-1985.*London 1986.

**Fish F :**
> *The London Hospital Dental School of the LHMC 1911-1991.* London 1991.

**Fraenkel G.J :**
> *Hugh Cairns, First Nuffield Professor of Surgery,* University of Oxford. OUP 1965.

**Gibbs D :**
> *Emblems, Tokens and Tickets of The London Hospital and The London Hospital Medical College.* London 1985.

**Gore J :**
> *Sydney Holland, Lord Knutsford. A memoir.* John Murray 1936.

**Grenfell W.T :**
> *Labrador Doctor.* Hodder and Stoughton London 1920.

**Holland S . Viscount Knutsford :**
> *In Black and White.* Edward Arnold London 1926.

**Howell M. and Ford P :**
> *The True History of the Elephant Man.* Penguin 1992.

**King A.C. and King A.J :**
> *Strong Medicine, Doctors at Home and Abroad.* Churchman 1990.

**Manton J :**
> *Elizabeth Garrett Anderson.* Methuen 1965,1986.

**Matron's Annual Letters :**
> 1894-1913. *E.Lückes.*
> 1922-1931. *B.M.Monk.*

**McEwan M :**
> *Eva C. Lückes.* LHLN London 1958.

**Morris E. W :**
> *The London Hospital.* Arnold and Co.London. 1st. Ed.1910. 3rd. Ed. 1926.

**Scott Stevenson R :**
> *Morrell Mackenzie. The Story of a Victorian Tragedy.* Heineman 1940.

**Treves F :**
> *The Elephant Man and other reminiscences.* Cassell London 1923.
> *Tales From a Field Hospital.* Cassell London 1900.

**Trombley S :**
> *Sir Frederick Treves - The Extra Ordinary Edwardian.* Routlege 1989.

**Wauchope G.M.W :**
> The Story of a Woman Physician. John Wright 1963.

# Appendix 1.   People and progress in the 20th. century.

| | |
|---|---|
| 1896. | -Hon. Sydney Holland elected chairman. Röntgen rays used in the Hospital. |
| 1898. | -Sir Frederick Treves retired. Payment for medicine and bandages for out-patients introduced. |

**The 1900's.**

| | |
|---|---|
| 1900. | -Medical College incorporated as a constituent school of the University of London. |
| 1901. | -Pathology Department built. |
| 1907. | -Arthur Keith, anatomist, and Martin Flack in the Medical College, with the assistance of James Mackenzie discovered the nervous mechanism of the heart, demonstrated in auricular fibrillation. This formed the scientific evidence on which the artificial pacemaker was developed later. |
| 1909. | - First Lady Almoner appointed later to become Medical Social Worker. |
| 1911. | -Lord Knutsford persuaded Sir James Mackenzie to join the Hospital staff, by providing a ward and the Department of Cardiology - the first such Department in Western Europe outside Paris. <br> -The Dental School was established; Professor Evelyn Sprawson, eminent scientist was a founder member, and director of dental studies from 1919 to 1946. |
| 1912. | -Dr. W. Wright, anatomist, Leonard Hill, physiologist and Dr.W. Bulloch, bacteriologist became professors of the University of London. <br> -Queen Alexandra opened rebuilt Tredegar House, as the Preliminary Training School for Nurses - the first in England when opened in 1895. |
| 1915 | -Edith Cavell entered in 1895, gained the London Hospital Certificate and left in 1901 to take posts elsewhere in England, before moving to Belgium, where she instituted an international nursing school thus influencing the development of nursing in Belgium. Her death, by firing squad on October 12th 1915, during the German occupation in the first world war, is marked each year by a wreath laying ceremony at the foot of her statue in Trafalgar Square. |

▲  *Edith Cavell (1865 - 1915)*

*1994 Wreath laying
by members of the current nursing staff.*

| | |
|---|---|
| 1919. | -Death of Miss Eva Lückes - Matron 1880-1919. <br> -Miss Beatrice Monk appointed Matron. She instituted The London Hospital Badge for Nurses, and The London Hospital League of Nurses in 1931 - the year she retired. |

**The 1920's.**

-Two annexes at Reigate were opened for surgical aftercare for patients transferred by ambulance from The London to reduce the pressure on the beds - then 849 in Whitechapel - the Croft Home 1920, for women, and Fairfield 1925, for men. Convalescence for women was provided at the Catherine Gladstone Home, Mitcham, and Morden Hall (maintained by Mr. Gilliat Hatfield) at Morden, Surrey. The Herman de Stern Convalescent Home for men at Felixstowe was supported by the Marie Celeste Samaritan Society. Later, after World War 11 this home provided convalescence for children referred by The London.

- The Medical Unit was established after World War 1, and amongst early research carried out in the unit were some of the first insulin trials in England in 1923, insulin having been discovered by Charles H. Best and Sir Frederick Grant Banting in 1921 - working in Macleod's Laboratory in Toronto.

1925.

-H M Queen Mary, President following the death of Queen Alexandra.
-Sir Henry Souttar-general surgeon, operated to stretch the mitral valve, and was the first to make use of radium at The London. He chose Hugh Cairns to be his house surgeon.

1926.

- Cairns gained a Rockefeller scholarship to study at Harvard University USA and after working with Harvey Cushing at the Johns' Hopkins Hospital in Boston USA, he returned to The London in 1927 to set up the new neurosurgical unit, and to introduce these pioneering techniques in brain surgery in Britain. After his appointment to the first Nuffield chair in surgery at the University of Oxford in the late 1930's, the neurosurgical work at The London was continued by Douglas Northfield, Jack Crawford and their successors.
-Neurology at The London began in the latter part of the 19th. century -with Sir Jonathan Hutchinson FRS, Dean of the Medical College, a distinguished physician, surgeon and authority on syphilis, working closely with Hughlings Jackson and later Sir Henry Head. It continued with George Riddoch and Russell Brain [ later Lord Brain.] These pioneers founded the basis for research and development in the neuro sciences for which the Hospital continues to be renowned.

1928.

-King George V seriously ill - operated on for empyema by Sir Hugh Rigby, Consultant Surgeon and nursed by London Hospital Sisters.

1929.

-Captain Henry Brierley appointed Steward. He became secretary in 1938 and House Governor in September 1939, a post he held until his retirement in 1962. A former officer in the Rifle Brigade in World War 1 he was a first rate administrator, with an amazing capacity for work. Single minded in his aim to enhance the reputation of The London, he was a constant source of strength and support to the hospital staff in changing times.

**The 1930's.**

1934.

- Queen Mary opened the Students' Hostel in Philpot Street which was later extended by the New Hall.

1936.

- School of Physiotherapy established.

1937.

-First private patients admitted to Fielden House.

1939.

- Evacuation to outlying hospitals in the Emergency Medical Services - the Sectors - on the out break of World War 11.

**The 1940's.**

1940/41.

-Blitz on East End and the docks.
-High explosive bombs damage the Lückes and Alexandra Nurses Homes, the laundry and Out-Patients' Department in September 1940 and the Medical College later in October 1940.
-Incendiary bombs and landmines bring further damage on the estate.
-King George VI and Queen Elizabeth visited The London to inspect war damage in the bi-centenary year.
-Zachery Merton Home, Banstead opened for rehabilitation and care of orthopoedic patients, medical or surgical patients with special needs. The Home closed in 1977.

| 1941 | -Miss Clare Alexander was appointed Matron. Her many achievements over ten years until she left in 1951 to marry Sir John Mann, Chairman, included:- the revision of the length of the patient's-day, the introduction of new methods of domestic supervision, a revised Study Day System for student nurses, and a new look for the traditional uniform for nursing staff due to wartime shortages, and clothing coupons. |
|---|---|
| 1941. | -The London Hospital Annexe Brentwood opened. |
| 1943. | -The Department of Industrial Medicine opened.<br>-Dr. Donald Hunter {1889-1978} consultant general physician, specialising in occupational health and disease.<br>-Department of Social Work established. |
| 1944. | -Accident and Orthopaedic Department opened - Sir Reginald Watson Jones, consultant orthopaedic surgeon.<br>-August 3rd., V.1.Rocket, flying bomb, destroyed a large section of the East Wing and the Institute of Pathology. |
| 1946. | -Queen Mary's Maternity Home, Hampstead became part of The London Hospital. |
| 1948. | -Last meeting of the House Committee on 28th. June 1948, and the dissolution of the Court of Governors instituted in 1740.<br>-New Board of Governors appointed by the Ministry of Health,under the chairmanship of Sir John Mann |
| 1949 | -Occupational Therapy Department opened. |

**The 1950's.**

| 1952. | -Death of King George VI, Patron. |
|---|---|
| 1953. | -Death of Queen Mary, President and Patron since 1925. H M Queen Elizabeth II graciously consented to become Patron, and visited in 1954. |
| 1957. | -Knutsford House, senior nursing staff residence opened, providing self contained flatlets, apart from the Nurses Homes.<br>-Research Laboratories in Ashfield Street opened.<br>- Hours of nursing staff reduced from 48 to 44 hours per week, and further reduced to 42 hours in 1966. |
| 1959 | Queen Alexandra's statue moved in May to face the Hospital. |

**The 1960's.**

| 1960. | -Sir John Mann retired as Chairman of the Board of Governors, and was appointed Vice-Patron in acknowledgement of his services to The London over 45 years. He died at his home in Norfolk on17th. September 1971.<br>-Mr Henry R. Moore succeeded Sir John as Chairman. He had become a governor in 1952 and Deputy Chairman in 1956. As Chairman of the Building Committee it was largely due to him that the re-building started in 1958.<br>-The 1960's were to see an expansion in both buildings and services.<br>Important contributions during the decade included:-<br>-a computer department,<br>-student accommodation in John Harrison House,<br>-a new Institute of Pathology,<br>-improved facilities for investigations in the Cardiac Department, and the provision of the Renal dialysis unit,<br>-Professor Roy Duckworth's research made an important contribution to dental health in children, leading to fluoridation. |
|---|---|

| 1961. | -Miss Phyllis Friend succeeded Miss G. Ceris Jones as Matron who left to become the Chief Nursing Officer of the Red Cross. In 1971, after her continuous service to the Red Cross, Miss Ceris Jones was presented by the Duke of Edinburgh with the Florence Nightingale Medal, the highest nursing award of the International Committee of the Red Cross. |
|---|---|
| 1962. | -Hon. John Scarlett Deputy House Governor succeeded Captain Brierley as House Governor. He retired after 26 years service to The London in 1972 and died in 1994.<br>The link block wards opened on August 3rd Bank holiday. |
| 1963 | -Lord Evans a well-known consultant physician at The London Hospital and physician to the nursing staff died on October 26th. He was physician to the Royal Household, a tradition extending from SirAndrew Clark in the nineteenth century.<br>John Harrison House opened. |
| 1964. | -Visit by H M The Queen. |
| 1965. | -The Dental Institute, Stepney Way opened.<br>-L.H. Drug Administration Chart adopted nationally. |
| 1967. | -On April 25th. 1967, Princess Alexandra opened the new nursing school building, to which she had graciously given her name. |
| 1968. | -Mile End Hospital and St. Clements Hospital designated to The London Hospital on April 1st. 1968 by the Minister of Health. |
| 1969 | The Board appointed Mr Sotiris Argyrou to promote collaboration between The London and representatives of local GPs and the staff of public health services provided by the local authority - pioneering work which was directed towards the achievement of an integrated health service for the East End. |

**The 1970's.**

| 1970. | -Closure of The London Hospital Annexe, Brentwood.<br>-Holland Wing opened.<br>-Demolition of the Old Alexandra Wing began. |
|---|---|
| 1971. | -Opening of 3 small residences for nursing staff in Philpot Street - by the Duchess of Kent - Dawson after Bertrand Dawson, Viscount Dawson of Penn (1864-1945), consultant physician to The London, and physician to the Royal Household, Horace Evans and Kent House. |
| 1972. | -Miss Phyllis Friend, Matron and Chief Nursing Officer, The London Hospital, received the insignia of Commander of the British Empire, in January 1972. She was Vice Chairman of the General Nursing Council for England and Wales and President of the Association of Hospital Matrons, and was the first member of staff of the NHS to attend the Administrative Staff College at Henley.<br>-Mr. Michael Fairey appointed House Governor on the retirement of Hon. John Scarlett CBE.<br>-Miss Margaret Day appointed Chief Nursing Officer at The London. Two years later she became District Nursing Officer Tower Hamlets on the 1974 NHS re- organisation, and retired in May 1985. |

**NHS Reorganisation Act 1974.**

| 1974. | -Board of Governors dissolved. Mr. H.R. Moore became Chairman and Mr Michael Fairey became regional administrator North East Thames Regional Health Authority.<br>- Mr Sotiris Argyrou appointed Area Administrator of the City & East London Health Authority, and Mr. David Kenny appointed District Administrator, Tower Hamlets, |
|---|---|
| 1975. | -Ashton House and Brierley House were occupied as staff residences in August - the official opening took place on June 29th. 1976 together with the flats in Clare Mann House. Ashton House was named after Sir Hubert Ashton, Vice Patron and member of the Board of Governors. |

| 1977. | -Two Nursing Research studies attracted external sponsorship - effective methods of communication, nursing care plans, and Ward Sister/learner interactions. |

1977.
-Two Nursing Research studies attracted external sponsorship - effective methods of communication, nursing care plans, and Ward Sister/learner interactions.

1978.
-Following research and developments between The London and Imperial College for joint repla ments, the Eurovision network televised Mr. Michael Freeman's total hip replacement to the Müller Institute in Berne Switzerland.
-Mr. Peter Chapple appointed District Administrator.

**The 1980's.**
-The Friends of The London Hospital (Whitechapel) established - a registered charity, with Lord Knutsford as President, Dr. Richard Bomford and Lord Delfont -Vice Presidents, and Mrs. Helen Taylor-Thompson as Chairman.

1981.
-Thanksgiving service at St. Paul's Cathedral on 24th October to mark the 50th. anniversary of the founding of The London Hospital League of Nurses, and the founding of The London Hospital Nursing School in 1873.

1982.
-On February 3rd.1982 the new Accident and Emergency Department came into use in Alexandra Wing, with a new central sterile supply department, and a suite of theatres named after Miss Margaret Kneale Jones Theatre Superintendent who died in December 1981.
-In March 1982 the Alexandra Wing was officially opened by H M The Queen.
-Mr. Francis Cumberlege appointed Chairman of Tower Hamlets District Health Authority (he was previously the Chairman of the Area Health Authority) and Sotiris Argyrou returned as District Administrator.
-18 months midwifery training began in line with European requirements.

1983.
-Relief of protracted pain-The L.H.M.C.Department of Therapeutics study (1978-83) was jointly financed by the North East Thames Region, Cancer Research and Cancer Relief. A London Hospital nurse and colleagues in the Department evolved The London Hospital Pain Observation Chart.

1984.
-Mile End Hospital -proposals for a purpose- built unit for the elderly agreed by the Region.
-Agreement for pre-clinical medical students' education between St. Bartholomew's, The London and Queen Mary and Westfield Colleges to go ahead.
-A Hospital Archivist appointed.

1985.
-The London Hospital Medical College celebrated its 200th. Anniversary - and the story of the growth of England's first medical school is told by John Ellis in "L.H.M.C. 1785-1985".
-Miss Margaret Day OBE retired May 1985.
-Dr A.E.Clark Kennedy, Dean of the Medical College 1937-1953, historian, died in September 1985.
-Occupational Health Service for all staff established.

1987.
-New gastro-enterology unit opened.David Wingate first professor of gastro - enterology, University of London.
-Princess Margaret visited part of the Hospital and the Medical College and became Patron of The League of Friends.
-Cambridge ward opened for Day Surgery.

1988.
-On October 19th. 1988, an English Heritage blue plaque commemorating Edith Cavell was unveiled on the wall of the Old Home.

1989.
-Amalgamation of The Princess Alexandra College of Nursing and Midwifery with those of Newham Health District.
-Centralisation of midwifery at Whitechapel.

**The 1990's.**
-The Neurosciences Department in Royal and Sophia wards and Oncology/Haematology in Knutsford Ward established.
-Visit of HM. The Queen July 5th. 1990 - opening the Trauma Unit, a new lift and helicopter landing pad on the roof of the Alexandra Wing - unveiling the inaugural plaque for the Children's

Unit, the Garden House, and conferring the title The Royal London Hospital.
-250th. Anniversary celebrations included:-A service of Thanksgiving and Rededication  at St. Paul's Cathedral on May 5th. 1990, The Anniversary Feast at The Guildhall-12th. June 1990, Participation in The Lord Mayor's Show,  November 1989.

1991.
-The Royal London Hospital and Associated Community NHS Trust formed on April 1st. 1991 under the Chairmanship of Sir William Staveley GCB CBIM, and Michael Fairey returning from the Department of Health as Chief Executive.
-Introduction of purchaser/provider financial systems nationally in the NHS.
-The Alexandra Staff Restaurant opened.
-The Garden House was opened by the Duke of Westminster on November 27th.1991.
-The Helicopter emergency medical service came into use - supported initially by  Express Newspapers.

1992
- Department of Quality Assurance developed.
-Clinical audit introduced on a multidisciplinary basis.
-April 1992, the Accident and Emergency Unit established by the Trust with a Head of Service, incorporating Admissions, Bed Management, Night Duty, the District Ambulance and the James Hora Hostel.One consultant, an experienced G.P. appointed to encourage collaboration between the Hospital and Primary Care.

1993.
-On January 1st. 1993, Sir William Staveley became Chairman of North East Thames Regional Health Authority.
-Mr. Michael Haines became Chairman of The Royal London NHS Trust.
-January 29th 1993 new day stay surgical unit opened.
-February 1993 Dr. Brian Mawhinney Minister of Health officially visited to open the Accident and Emergency Department.
-In February 1993 the Government issued "Making London Better", its response to Professor Sir Bernhard Tomlinson's report (1992) on London's Health Service.
-April 1993, the Chairman of the prospective merged trust was announced - Lieutenant General Sir Derek Boorman KCB.
-In June 1993, a Project Steering Group was appointed to draw up plans for the new Trust.

1994
-April1st.1994. The Royal Hospitals Trust was formed by the merger of three hospitals - The Royal Hospital of Saint Bartholomew, The Royal London Hospital, and The London Chest Hospital.
Sir Derek became Chairman and Mr. Gerry Green was appointed Chief Executive.

# Appendix 11.   Matrons.

| | |
|---|---|
| 1740-1741. | The first matron in Featherstone Street was Mrs. Ann Looker, wife of the porter. Both were dismissed for stealing a year later in1742. |
| 1742-1757. | Mrs. Elizabeth Broad was elected as Matron for the Houses in Prescot Street. She died in 1757 three months before the new hospital in Whitechapel was opened. The House Committee Minutes (1757) record "her great fidelity". |
| 1742-1745. | Mrs. Elizabeth Gilbert was also elected as Matron for "the Lock" - the Prescot Street house for patients with venereal disease, which remained separated from the Infirmary patients. |
| 1745-1763. | She was succeeded by Mrs. Mary Gouy in 1745. The House later became the Magdalen Hospital for Penitent Prostitutes in 1758, and at this point Mrs. Gouy moved to the new building in Whitechapel, until her death in 1763. There were two matrons - one for the East End and one for the West End of the new building - for many years until, due to financial difficulties in 1782 it was resolved that when one matron left, an assistant matron should be sought for due economy. |
| 1757-1769. | Mrs Joanna Martin was appointed Matron of the Hospital. On her election, she was "given leave to go to her usual place of worship on Sunday as she was a dissenter". |
| 1769-1788. | Mrs. Patterson was elected Matron of the West End of the Hospital, but in 1781 she was put in charge of the whole building for a year as the other Matron, Mrs. Stainbank (1776-1790) had fractured her leg. Mrs. Patterson was "granted 1 week's leave in the country for the preservation of her health each year." In 1788 the House Committee "resolved that, in view of her great age and long and faithful service Mrs. Patterson be permitted to resign and allowed £15 p.a. during pleasure". |
| 1790. | When Mrs. Stainbank died advertisements were "placed in the Public Gazetteer, the Ledger and the Daily Record daily, and on different days for the appointment and election of Matron, and a General Court to be summoned". Mrs. Ann Guion was appointed. |
| 1798-1804. | Mrs. Arabella Donne accepted office on 16th.January 1798. The House Committee determined on March 13th. 1798 that "The Matron's two rooms to be painted and prepared with paper at 5 pence per yard" Mrs. Donne resigned on 5th. June 1804. |
| 1804-1833. | Miss Catherine Le Blond was called to the House Committee on June 26th. 1804, "her duty read to her, and she was admitted." She left in 1833. |
| 1833-1867. | Mrs Jane Nelson-previously Matron,Westmoreland Hospital, Dublin. |
| 1867-1880. | Miss. Annie Maria Swift-previously Mrs. Nelson's Assistant 1862-1867. |
| 1880-1919. | Miss Eva Lückes CBE, RRC, Lady of Grace, Order of St.John.- trained at Westminster Hospital, night sister at The London 1879, Lady Superintendent, Pendlebury Childrens' Hospital for six months until February 1880. |
| 1919-1931. | Miss Beatrice M. Monk, CBE, RRC.- trained The London Hospital, Assistant Matron, and Steward The London Hospital 1918/1919. |
| 1931-1938. | Miss A.M.Littleboy-trained The London Hospital. Assistant Matron. |
| 1938-1939. | Miss Mabel Reynolds-trained The London Hospital. In 1939, Matron Sector 1, EMS. |
| 1939-1941. | Miss Alice K. Burgess-Acting Matron. Trained The London Hospital-Assistant Matron. |
| 1941-1951. | Miss Clare Alexander, CBE. -trained The London Hospital, Senior Sister Tutor The London Hospital, Matron Addenbrookes Hospital Cambridge 1938/41. |
| 1951-1961. | Miss Gwyneth Ceris Jones. - trained at The Nightingale School, tutor Addenbrooke's, |

Assistant Matron The London Hospital, Matron Westminster Hospital.

1961-1971.       MissPhyllis Friend, CBE.  Matron/Chief Nursing Officer.-trained The London Hospital, Assistant Matron St. George's Hospital. Miss Friend left in 1971 to become the Chief Nursing Officer, Department of Health, England, later Dame of British Empire.

1972- 1974.      Miss Margaret Day. Chief Nursing Officer.-The London Hospital. trained Guy's Hospital School of Nursing.

1972-1983       Miss M. Culpeck, Matron ( Divisional Nursing Officer ) Whitechapel, trained The London Hospital.

1974-1985.      Miss Margaret Day. OBE. District Nursing Officer, Tower Hamlets' Health District.

1983-1986       Miss M. Scholes, Director of Nursing Service, Whitechapel, trained The London Hospital.

1985-1986.      Miss Margaret Deadman. Acting  District Nursing Officer Tower Hamlets Health  District.- trained The London Hospital, Assistant Matron The Wellington Hospital.

1986-1991.      Miss Lynette Harding Chief Nursing Officer / Nursing Adviser Tower Hamlets' District Health Authority. Trained The London Hospital.

1986-1988       Miss M. Scholes - Clinical Facilities Manager, Whitechapel.

1988-1991       Miss B. Faulkner - Clinical Facilities Manager, Whitechapel, trained Guy's Hospital.

**The Royal London Hospital and Associated Community NHS Trust.**

1991-1994.      Miss Trudy Wood. Director of Nursing  and Quality Assurance. trained The London  Hospital.

**The Royal London Hospitals  NHS Trust.**

1994-         Miss Pamela Hibbs OBE,  Chief Nurse and Director of Quality Assurance - trained St Bartholomew's  Hospital.

# INDEX

Given below are the names of the principal people and places as they appear in the text